POETRY FOR THE
AWAKENING
2

The Lion Within

Vanessa Bristow-Rose

Cover Artwork
by
Abigail Barker

Illustrations
by
Sophie Wright

The Lion Within

First published in the UK June 2014 by MyVoice Publishing

Cover Artwork by Abigail Barker
Illustrations by Sophie Wright

Published by: MyVoice Publishing,
33 -34 Mountney Bridge Business Park
Westham
PEVENSEY
BN24 5NJ

www.myvoicepublishing.co.uk

ISBN: 978-1-909359-24-6

*This book is dedicated to my
beloved sister, Rowena,
whose spirit is with me
constantly from 'the other side',
whose guidance I value.
Bless you my dear sister,
I miss your physical presence.*

*Also to all lightworkers,
wherever you are.
You are the army of light,
bringing hope and love
in abundance to the planet
we call home, and to all
who dwell and live upon her.
Wherever you are and whatever
your role in the journey of light,
I offer you all my humble gratitude.
Namaste to each and every one of you.*

The Lion Within

II

About The Author

Vanessa is the youngest child of a family of two daughters. She was born in the spring of 1958 in Woolwich, London. Although born in England, Vanessa spent the first 9 years of her life in East Africa. Arriving in Mbarara, Uganda at the tender age of six weeks, she spent all of her infancy there until moving onto Dar Es Salaam, Tanzania at the age of 6 years. After only a year there, and after suffering three separate attacks of malaria, Vanessa and her family moved to Nairobi, Kenya. The higher altitude proved better for Vanessa's health and the family remained there until 1967. This was an idyllic childhood with the freedom to explore nature and the opportunity to grow up in another culture, which was so fundamentally based on community living and closeness to family. There will always be a part of her heart belonging to Africa.

Vanessa's family moved to Georgetown, Guyana, South America in 1968 and just before her 11th birthday, she was sent back to England to be a boarder at Pipers Corner School in Great Kingshill near High Wycombe. Vanessa found it a difficult and challenging experience being so far away from her immediate family. However, she had many positive experiences too and was fortunate to be able to spend Easter holidays and half term breaks with extended family near Oxford.

After two years at college in Hastings, East Sussex Vanessa left with an O.N.D. (Ordinary National Diploma) in Business Studies and secretarial skills. Still with no idea what to do for a career, she held a couple of brief temporary jobs until she joined Sussex Police as a Police Officer in 1978. This gave her an extended insight into the varying aspects of human nature and was the beginning of the realisation that not all in our world is as presented by mainstream media. She became ill in 2005/2006 after exposure to microwave radiation from mobile phones, dect phones but by far the most intensive exposure was from Tetra Airwave, adopted by the police to update their communications from UHF and VHF radio systems. She left work after being diagnosed with Hashimoto's Thyroiditis. (For further information see www.mercola.com). Thus another awakening to the realisation that despite the clear evidence that Tetra Airwave had negative health effects on biological beings, the corporations producing it and the authorities adopting it were in denial. The poem 'Death Towers' covers this issue. Also, please refer to the Appendix at the back of this book for information on websites exploring this issue.

Vanessa now lives in East Sussex and her hobbies include walking in the countryside, especially wild places, writing and music. She plays the Great Highland Bagpipes, Gongs and the Native American Flute. Vanessa has been writing poetry for family and friends since 1982, mainly for their enjoyment and for fun.

In the last couple of years, her poetry has changed direction and has become more spiritual in nature. Now, questioning of the state of the world and the many things which are unjust, corrupt and destructive, there rises a compulsion to write and to shine a light on these issues so that they can no longer hide in the shadows of obscurity and secrecy. Whilst much of the beauty of our world is found in the abundant diversity which exists around and amongst us, there are some things about life here on Earth which need exposing and addressing for the sake of all humankind. Vanessa is often inspired by events around her and by the reading of books and websites on wide and thought provoking subjects (detailed references to these sources are available in the Appendix).

It is with love that the poetry within this book has been written and it is hoped that the contents will inspire and encourage the reader to explore further into the mysteries and magic of the world in which we live. It is the author's belief that the future for humankind and all other beings on planet Earth, is a glorious and wonderful one and it is hoped that the poems within this book will reflect that. There is no expectancy that the reader accepts Vanessa's view of the world, but she encourages the reader to question further and enquire more deeply into the subjects raised in this book. The Appendix at the back of this book has been provided to assist this process and to show where the inspiration has come from for some of the poems.

Vanessa is also the author of the first book in this series 'Poetry for the Awakening'.

Thank you for choosing this book. May it bring you joy on your journey of discovery.

The Lion Within

Introduction

This is a time on Earth which is challenging. So much harm has been done to this beloved planet we call home, that it fills the heart with sadness. Everywhere you turn there is exploitation of the Earth's resources, her skin ripped open to expose her hidden treasures. Her skies are polluted from industrial waste, chemtrails, nuclear testing and microwave radiation from cell phone towers. Her waters are tainted and poisoned from industrial accidents, chemical waste discharges and a myriad of other sources.

It would be easy to point the finger at humanity and to hold it collectively responsible for this mess. Blame them for the degradation and destruction of the forests and rivers. Whilst there is unquestionably a need to take responsibility, and to remember our ancestors teachings with regard to honouring our planet and all living things which dwell upon her, let us not lose sight of the greed of multi-national corporations who talk words of saving the ecology, whilst at the same time continuing with the endless extraction of resources and provoking wars for their own profit.

Governments make promises and spout words of placation to the concerned public, but nothing really changes. Endless petitions have been signed and submitted to governments. Numerous demonstrations by caring people stating their concerns on placards have marched the street. Mountains of letters have been sent in protest about the continuous violation of human rights and corrupt exploitation by corporations.

Enough is enough. Change will happen when we, the people and guardians of this planet, take back our power and act for love and betterment of all humankind and all other sentient beings of this beautiful planet we call Earth.

I would like to open with some words which came to me through automatic writing during a meditation in July 2011. They are food for thought I think.

Frequency brings light energy to the world and all colours exist in every musical note.
The Universe calls to us to speak our truth.
Love connects everything together,
yet we do not see the golden threads of love and light holding all things together as One.
Nothing separate survives for long.
There is an interdependence with all things.

*When I asked why we are here the answer which came back was **"You are expressions of the Divine breath and you are here to breath love back into the Web."***

"I believe that unarmed truth and unconditional love will have the final word in reality."

Dr Martin Luther King

"When the power of love overcomes the love of power, the world will know peace."

Jimi Hendrix

The Lion Within

X

Contents

About The Author	III
Introduction	VII
The Lion Within	3
Prayer	5
What Am I?	6
Soul Of The Light	7
I'm Thinking Of You	9
Communities Of Light	12
Silent Sound	14
Innit!	16
Mother Instinct	18
Earth's Heart Chakra	20
Soul Raven	23
Humanity United	25
My Gentle Child	26
Clean The Body Vehicle Out	28
One Earth	30
Jessie's Trust	33
Peace, It Appears, Is Missing	35
Angelic Pipes And Drums	37
Born From Light	39
What's This Fracking?	42
Creative Thought	45
Sing With The Angels	47
The Mouse And The Gnome	49
A Tree's Story Of Love	51
When I Look Into Your Eyes	54
Poison Sky	55
Earth Angels	57
I Win...You Lose	60
All That Is	62
War Horse	64
Crop Circles	66

The Lion Within

The Spirit Of Yew	69
I Wonder Where You Are	73
Earth's Child	76
Best Friend	78
Imagine	81
Death Towers	83
What If....It's An Illusion?	86
Ubuntu	89
Only Love Resides Here	90
Taking The Piss	92
The Awakening Police	94
Hector The Dragon	98
Appendix	101

"Rise like lions after slumber
in unvanquishable number,
Shake your chains to earth like dew
which in sleep had fallen on you -
Ye are many - they are few."

Percy Bysshe Shelley – The Mask of Anarchy

The Lion Within

Vanessa Bristow-Rose

The Lion Within

I yearn for the scent
of the Rift Valley trees;
The acacia and euphorbia,
swaying in the dry breeze.
Oh Africa....the ancient home
of my ancestors....so long gone.
Their wisdom is still honoured,
for their spirit lives on.
The elevated rocks
where, as a cub, I once played.
Within the pride of my family,
I never felt afraid.
We would lie in the shade
away from the sun's heat,
not until it was cooler
would we hunt, play and eat.

Now, my horizon is filled
with high chain-link fencing.
This part-concrete enclosure
feels unfriendly and menacing.
Here to be looked at,
my freedom curtailed,
to see me in my magnificence
you have horribly failed.
If you looked into my eyes
you would see hopelessness there,
the pain of lost freedom
my soul cannot bear.

The Lion Within

Where once there was resistance,
resignation resides.
I am heavy in my heart
where a deep sorrow hides.
There's a depression in my roar,
why have you not heard?
You have caged up my soul
like clipping wings of a bird.
Perhaps my service here
is to help you to see,
you have done to yourself
what you have done to me.
The lion within <u>you</u>
is imprisoned....not free.
All is ONE
in the infinite energy sea.
From centuries of trauma
your heart has been sealed,
only love penetrates through
the karmic effect shield.
Too late for my release.
I'm ready to pass
over to the kingdom
of golden trees and grass.
But awaken dear people,
for my children and theirs.
Let their eyes behold Africa
and their hearts be free of cares.
When we all remember
that truly we're all ONE,
we will honour each Being's freedom
under God's sacred sun.

"*There is a power inside every human against which no earthly force is of the slightest consequence.*"

Neville Goddard

Prayer

Dear beloved lion within.
The lion within me.
The lion I have imprisoned,
Now I set you free.

Dear beloved lion within.
United we will be.
Lion who dwells within my heart,
Our strength will set us free.

What Am I?

I am vast in mass and distance,
in length and depth and width.
I have existed since time began,
I'm in poem, book and myth.
All beings love me
and everyone intimately engages.
Influenced by cold, heat and wind
my structure for ever changes.

The light..it dances through me
and I reflect what is around.
A mirror am I when all is still,
I'm in the sky, the air and ground.
White horses dance upon my head
and sands roll beneath my feet.
My belly carries cetacean beings.
It's where they live and sing and meet.

The continents of Planet Earth
they all know me well,
we have existed side by side,
much history we could tell.
I am her life-blood,
energy flowing to every part,
bringing light onto the Earth
to caress her sacred heart.

It is easy now to see who is ME.
I am the water of the ever-changing sea.

Soul Of The Light

Soul of the Light
step up and claim your power.
Your strength will be needed
for Earth's critical hour.
For you, dear spirit
of all divine light,
are a star from the heavens
sent to shine on Earth bright.

Soul of the Light
now you know who you are,
a part of the Oneness,
an eternal star.
All that has bound you
to this earthly place,
will fade in the brilliance
of your gentle grace.

Soul of the Light
sing gently..to those souls
who have lost their way
and sight of their goals.
Spread your light
with compassion and love.
For we are all ONE
to the Creator above.

Soul of the Light,
blessed child of the universe,
you have had thousands of lives
to prepare and rehearse
for this mighty moment
of the Dark's final fight,
and help secure Earth's ascension
and her people to divine Light.

Espavo
(thank you for taking your power)

Vanessa Bristow-Rose

I'm Thinking Of You

(Lyrics)

I'm thinking of you,
my dear special friend.
You have flown with the angels
back to heaven again.
Thank you for being
the person you are,
though you have gone,
I know it's not far.

I hear your sweet voice,
it floats on the breeze.
Closing my eyes,
I can picture you with ease.
I hold out my hand
and I'm sure that I feel
your hand holding mine,
for the touch is so real.

I know that my missing you
is because I can't see,
your beautiful face
smiling back at me.

I'm thinking of you,
my dear special friend.
My love and my gratitude
to you I will send.
I'm so very glad
that you and I met.
A gentle soul like you
I never will forget.

Please save me a place
in God's paradise too,
so that when I get to heaven
again, I'll see you.
Thank you for the memories
that knowing you brings.
There's a new soul in heaven
that's why an angel sings.

I'm thinking of you,
my dear special friend,
of your joy at returning
to Heaven's home again.

I'm Thinking of You

Vanessa Bristow-Rose

I'm think-ing of you, my dear spe-cial friend. You have flown with the an-gels back to hea-ven a-gain.

Thank you for be-ing the per-son you are, though you have gone, I know it's not far. I hear your sweet

voice, it floats on the breeze. Clos-ing my eyes, I can pic-ture you with ease. I hold out my hand & I'm

sure that I feel your hand hold-ing mine, for the touch is so real. I know that my mis-sing you is be

cause I can't see, your beau-ti-ful face smil-ing back at me. I'm think-ing of you, my dear spe-cial

friend. My love & my gra-ti-tude to you I will send. I'm so ve-ry glad that you & I met, a

gen-tle soul like you I ne-ver will for-get. Please save me a place in God's pa-ra-dise too, so that

when I get to hea-ven a-gain, I'll see you. Thank you for the mem-o-ries that know-ing you brings. There's a

new soul in hea-ven that's why an an-gel sings. I'm think-ing of you, my

dear spe-cial friend, of your joy at re-turn-ing to Hea-ven's home a-gain.

Communities Of Light

Bringing in the communities of light,
is what we came to do.
A transition from a duality world,
to a more enlightened view.
Where everyone is equal
and suffering is not known.
The pain of never feeling loved
is an experience quite unknown.

An advanced respect for all that lives
because of divine connection,
to all that ever has existed
and to the ONE of all creation.
The building of light communities
may seem an awesome task.
Many light beings are here
to help us, we only have to ask.

Before any structure can take its shape
in this physical dimension,
to visualise the world we would see
must be clear in our comprehension.
For we are all creators
and our reality we create,
so better built on the strength of love
than more division, fear and hate.

The seed of love can take its root
in the tiniest of places.
It will dissolve division which has existed
between all races.

The flame of love can soon become
a roaring, blazing fire,
igniting every heart it touches
to blossom with desire.

From the flower of unconditional love,
many fruits will spawn.
Abundance, peace and creativity
will help bring the dream to form.
Crystal spires and domes of quartz
glow with radiance in the sun.
Shimmering pinks and glistening golds
emanate from the consciousness of ONE.

This radiance of human love
is in every community's aura.
Its brilliance pulsating,
in every animal, form and flora.
Central to each community
lies the community's inner heart.
There stands a crystal pyramid
vibrating cosmic energy to every part.

The bloom of light from a community's heart
will beam up into space.
A signal to the cosmos
of humanity's progress as a race.
Awakening to the light we are,
to the 'I AM' that is within,
for when we embrace this sacred truth
the Golden Age can begin.

Silent Sound

There is a world beyond the noise.
There is a world of silence.
It exists beyond the realms of sound,
outside our familiarity of experience.
Observe the stillness in the pause,
between every word that's spoken.
Truth exists within the space
where silence is unbroken.

A whirling, swirling potentiality
in a vibrational, soundless sea.
Memories of what everything was,
dreams of what could possibly be.
The quiet trees stand in silent witness
to endless human death and pain.
And what of the elusive peace
that's hidden within the human brain?

We think we understand past truth,
through being 'taught' our history.
But real truth lies in the Akashic records
of the eternal energy sea.
Listen with your body cells.
Listen with your heart.
Between the beats resides a knowingness
that we are never souls apart.

From the vastness of the All That Is,
and in the stillness of our sleep,
our very essence surfaces
whilst we are dreaming deep.
If we stop for just a moment
from the frenzied rush and tear,
then in the stillness we will discover
what nature wants to share.

For all around us on Earth's plane,
exists an invitation to listen.
To quieten down our busy lives,
taking time to create a vision.
Catch the joyous noise of peace
and within it we will find,
the visions and dreams of a newer world
of the compassionate, loving kind.

Innit!

They meet in the heavens
those angels of light.
To play their instruments
and have fun......right?
They're bringing their bagpipes
and drumming kit.
Their intention's to create
healing sound......innit?!

Starting off quietly
they play on the chanter.
It's an illusion for the noise
they'll develop soon after.
Standing in a circle
for the practice requisite.
Warming those bagpipes
is a deafening din......innit?!

Not being incarnate
has advantages......see?
Because physical bodies
get tired easily.
Angels play for hours,
they don't have to be fit.
Not out of puff once!
It's remarkable......innit?!

Now humans, you see,
they're blowing and moaning.
In just thirty minutes,
they're tired and groaning.
They've got to have puff.
They've got to be fit.
Because it's hot
sweaty work......innit?!

Angels don't tire
in their heavenly service,
weaving their music
for eternal bliss.
Never exhausted.
They don't have to sit.
It's great having
endless energy......innit?!

Hear them in the valleys
and on the mountains high.
Cleansing with their music
all the land and sky.
Thousands of pipers
with music exquisite.
Lovely with
earplugs in though......innit?!

Mother Instinct

When a young creature is orphaned
it is warming to see,
that others come to offer
what help they could be.
But when there's no-one
of your species, of your kind,
to surrogate for the nurturing,
how, a mother, do you find?

The mothering instinct is the melody
of the Creator's song.
It is the urge to protect,
the need to nurture
an infant which is strong.
This can cross all the boundaries
between species of Being,
to honour the need
for survival of the living.

Stories abound of such
heroic rescue deeds,
all done on an impulse
to serve another's needs.
Dolphins, for instance,
have supported in the sea
people they've saved from
a drowning catastrophe.

There is an energy
which unites the species divide.
It is the field of 'All That Is'
within which we all reside.
By helping each other
in true compassionate action,
we help ourselves also
through the field of connection.

It's the ripple effect
of all that we do.
Love resolves everything,
recreating our world new.
The Mother Instinct is powerful;
it is a form of love.
It ensures each species evolution
into the higher realms above.

Earth's Heart Chakra

It's a spiral of energy.
It's a vortex of love.
Earth's pure heart connects
to the sacred heart above.
Love resonance waves
like ripples in a pond,
fan out into the sky,
the universe and beyond.

Each human heart,
if its resonance is strong,
will synchronise rhythm
with the ONE cosmic song.
Planet Earth's heart
beats in Glastonbury, UK.
The signal pulses out
to the whole milky way.

Her heart chakra projects
its healing pink light,
which, as it's tuned into love,
glows boldly and bright.
No negative energies,
no entities and no fear
can penetrate or extinguish
Earth's love energy sphere.

Vanessa Bristow-Rose

Uniting our hearts with
her own unique beat,
the love will flood over
ensuring the dark reigns defeat.
The frequency of love
is the song for the soul,
to find its way back
to the ONE and be whole.

So gather in thousands
in Earth's sacred places,
all peoples, all colours,
nations and races.
An electromagnetic surge
will bless all the Earth,
cleansing and purifying
her ready for re-birth.

Soul Raven

Circling and swooping
and gliding with ease.
Flying like an acrobat
over the tops of the trees.
Dancing in rhythm
to the wind's flowing breath.
Spiralling and twisting
in defiance of death.

Silken sleek body
framed by blue sky.
The Earth smiles gently
as she watches him fly.
With wings widely spread
he darts left and right.
Nature's creation
is perfection in flight.

The sun reflects brightly
off dark glossy feather.
The wind's buoyant bluster
uplifts him in all weather.
Such grace in the dance
of the raven of light.
The skill he possesses
is his God gifted birthright.

Bound to Earth's bosom
by an invisible cord,
there's an energy connecting
everything in unified accord.
No cage for him though,
no border patrols,
it's how it should be
for all living souls.

There is only one Being
on the planet of Earth,
which imprisons itself
from the moment of birth.
Creating countries and borders
with passport controls,
systems of governance
to enslave human souls.

Divided and subjugated
we are no longer free.
With the wings of our souls clipped
we cease to see,
that unity will release us,
our souls free to soar,
to move without hindrance
across all land, sea and shore.

Vanessa Bristow-Rose

Humanity United

Humanity truly are sparks of divine light.
Unity is how we will bring the world right.
Merging together, all people unite.
And by sharing with compassion our hearts will ignite.
No more separation. We can love and not fight.
Imagine our Earth then. What an incredible sight.
Together our love will overpower the night.
You and I united can create our future bright.

Undoing past wrongs, putting everything right.
Negate all of science denying our spiritual insight.
Integrate free energy for affordable light.
Teach all the children of their true divine birthright.
End all division, as ONE family we re-unite.
Delivered from slavery we can ascend to the light.

"A house divided against itself cannot stand."

Abraham Lincoln

My Gentle Child

(Lyrics)

<u>**Chorus**</u>
My gentle child can you not see
That I am you and you are me.
My gentle child can you not see
All is as it's meant to be.

Who am I? I hear your plea.
So alone you call to me.
Lonely because you cannot see.
You are the light. Your soul is free.
You are the clouds. You are the sky.
You are the birds flying high.
You are the mountains, rocks and sand,
A part of all Earth's sacred land.

Chorus

Open your eyes and you will see
The truth as it will always be.
You are the waves, rivers and sea.
You're every creature, plant and tree.
My dearest child there's no apart.
For you are my own loving heart.
We are connected, a united ONE,
The universe, planets, stars and sun.

Chorus

My Gentle Child

Vanessa Bristow-Rose

My gen-tle child can you not see that I am you & you are me. My gen-tle child can you not see

all is as its meant to be. Who am I? I hear your plea. So a-lone you call to me. Lone-ly be-cause you

can-not see. You are the light. Your soul is free. You are the clouds. You are the sky. You are the birds

fly-ing high. You are the moun-tains, rocks & sand, a part of all earths sa-cred land. My gen-tle child can

you not see that I am you & you are me. My gen-tle child can you not see all is as it's meant to be.

Op-en your eyes & you will see, the truth as it will al-ways be. You are the waves, ri-vers & sea. You're

eve-ry crea-ture, plant & tree. My dear-est child there's no a-part, for you are my own lov-ing heart. We

are con-nect-ed, a u-nit-ed ONE, the u-ni-verse, pla-nets, stars & sun. My gen-tle child can

you not see that I am you & you are me. My gen-tle child can you not see all is as it's meant to be.

Clean The Body Vehicle Out

Now is the time to clear
those dusty corners and shelves.
Let the fresh air of joy
filter through into ourselves.
Those shadows lurking deep within
the pathways of our mind
which, for years, have blocked the light
and routinely undermined.

Self-doubt has been an invisible chain
to restrain us from expansion.
Self-condemnation is another beast
which usurps and steals our vision.
Clean the body vehicle out
until every part is bright.
The chakras clear and spinning,
with the energies flowing right.

The journey begins by flushing out
all the sticky ancient dross.
The energies stuck from all the lives
of grieving, pain and loss.
It is the time to heal the soul,
to be courageous, brave and bold.
Call upon the angels strong
to cut the bondage cords of old.

For too long we have succumbed,
to the belief we are not enough.
Have unwittingly consented
to be limited by lies and stuff.
Clear out the clutter...
those dark entities hiding within.
You have the power to do it.
For the light will always win.

Years of guilt and fear
serve no purpose any more.
We are freed by using our own will.
It is the universal law.
You are a divine being of light.
Your power lies in your soul.
Call upon your Higher Self
in your journey to be whole.

By lifting our vibration
we will heal our Earth mother.
The work is swift when we are ONE
....dearest sister and brother.
A sovereign child of the Earth Goddess,
the child of a cosmic star.
All will be revealed to you
when you remember who you are.

One Earth

ONE Earth........
A planet circling in our universe,
our solar system.
A blue sapphire sphere
spinning in rhythm,
teaming with life in her seas,
land and air.
A jewel of creation
that all life forms share.

ONE Land........
But divided into countries
with borders.
No freedom to roam.
Bound by rules, laws and orders.
Denied access for many,
whilst others we displace.
Refugees in their thousands
is an outrageous disgrace.

ONE Sea........
Yet carved up by more
invisible borders.
Divided and patrolled
by military marauders.
We should learn from the water,
the creatures of the sea,
who ignore human boundaries
moving everywhere free.

ONE Humanity........
Yet separated by race,
creed and culture.
Why not embrace differences?
Learning to nurture.
The conduct of every one
influences us all.
More division, hate and racism
ensures humanity's fall.

ONE Nation........
Split apart by different beliefs,
and further compounded
by self-interested Chiefs.
Often there's an unwillingness
to compromise and share.
Leading to war, endless conflict
and a profound lack of care.

ONE Family........
Every animal and plant,
bird and tree
is linked through the energy field,
to Gaia's land and sea.
It's an illusion
that we are individuals apart.
We are each connected
to the great Divine heart.

ONE Consciousness........
Reminds us to return to unity.
Joining hearts in compassion,
love restoring humanity.
For love is the pathway,
leading us back to the Source.
Love returns us to paradise
as a matter of course.

"I have no country to fight for;
my country is the Earth,
and I am a citizen of the world."

Eugene V. Debs

Vanessa Bristow-Rose

Jessie's Trust
(A dalmation's story)

Once born I telepathically called to you,
and then you did appear.
Recognition ignited my soul with joy
to see you here.
I know that I'm meant to be with you,
it's a knowledge deep in my heart.
We are destined to share our lives together,
for our souls cannot be apart.

We are soul-friends twinned forever,
over aeons we have been.
Sharing side by side
through Earth's changing movie screen.
I have to help you find me,
for you have forgotten our pre-birth plan.
Then once we are reunited
I will help you all I can.

So pick me please, I beg you,
from the puppies you came to see.
The skill is how to help you
see the most awesome pup is me!
My sister snuggled in your arms,
though a beautiful puppy too,
is not the one that God, with love,
has allocated you.

I'm here to help and guide you.
I'm an angel in disguise.
Although I'm in a doggie suit
I'm very old and wise.
You may be dazzled by my spots,
God's special gift of polka dots.
They are a message given to me,
to help you remember,
to help you see...

That I am of the heavenly light,
reflected in my coat of white.
God gave me spots because he cared,
to remind you of the many lives we've shared.
Your belief in loving kindness
and all that's fair and just
is why I, JESSIE, have in you
absolute faith and TRUST.

Vanessa Bristow-Rose

Peace, It Appears, Is Missing

Peace, it appears, is missing.
Has anybody seen her?
So many places now on Earth
where Peace will never enter.
In this destructive, crazy world
I've been looking far and wide.
But dear beloved Peace,
has run away to hide.

Please tell me you've seen Peace.
She's been missing for a while.
Without her valiant presence,
humanity's enslaved and put on trial.
She won't be where the cameras
watch our every move,
for surveillance is controlling
and Peace would not approve.

Please help me to find Peace.
She'll be with her other friends.
Harmony and Freedom accompany her,
they are where all tyranny ends.
Peace will not be found near war,
nor where people starve;
where there are poor.

The Lion Within

Please tell me you've seen Peace,
for it's where our future lies.
When humanity finds Peace,
that is when suppression dies.
Peace will never linger long
where injustice rules
and inequality is strong.

Please join with me to find her.
A unified effort we will need.
When Peace sees we will defend her,
humanity will be freed.
Peace must be protected,
for she stands for absolute truth.
We must rediscover Peace
for all our future youth.

But if Peace is really missing
then where does the search begin?
It's then we might discover
that, in truth, she dwells within.

Angelic Pipes And Drums

Should you look across the Highlands
and be dazzled by the light.
A halo on the horizon,
etheric, bold and bright.
Close your eyes and listen
for the music that will come,
across the breeze to kiss your ears
of angelic pipe and drum.

For they march across the land,
those angels thousands strong,
to sweep the earth before them
with music and with song.
This blessed army of angels
flow across the war-torn soil.
Cleansing, using sacred sound,
where men fight and die and toil.

No stone is left untouched.
No heather left unclean.
Bagpipes woven in with drum
to purify the scene.
So they weave their love
through music,
over loch and hill and tor.
Peace descends like a soft caress
where once was pain and war.

The earth upon which these angels tread
is glowing brilliant white.
All negative energies transmuted
and returned into the light.
These angels, in their legions,
hold high the violet flame,
to clear the energy of war,
of death and fear and maim.

Every note the angels play
is imbued with a violet glow.
Every seed of joyous sound
sown with love will grow.
These angels are light warriors,
not soldiers, marines or snipers,
with only sacred instruments
they are the Heaven's Pipers.

Born From Light

A Being is born from light.
Electromagnetic frequencies
dancing to love's rhythms.
Seeded across time
from far away sentient star systems.
Pure heavenly music
weaving the harmonic of love's creation,
stimulates cells to replicate
into unified perfection.
Nurtured within the mother's womb.
Supported by the elixir
of creation's essences,
the child develops at-one-ment
to the world through all senses.
Bathed in the warm waters,
infused with muffled sound,
the infant is sensitive
to the vibrations that surround.
All things experienced
by the mother Being outside,
will impact energetically
on the developing one inside.
Every emotion is shared
simultaneously by them both.
All fear, resentment and anger
will affect the child's growth.
Experiences are stored
in each cell's field of energy
and can remain there as triggers
of response in personality.
Send love to the infant

and vibrations of joy.
Play beautiful music
for the ears to enjoy.
Then that frequency of thought
will reach to the heart,
to give the body
a high love-energy start.
Surrounding the baby
in joy, peace and love
will keep the pineal open
to cosmic connections above.

Vanessa Bristow-Rose

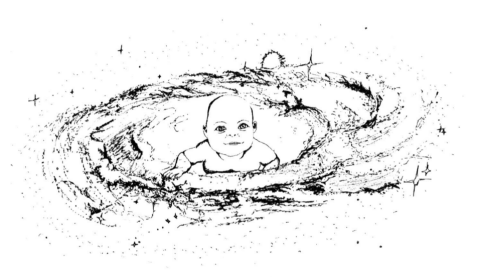

What's This Fracking?

What's this 'fracking'
being done to our beloved Mother Earth?
Squeezing her of all resources,
robbing her for all they're worth.
Drilling thousands of feet
beneath the ground.
Yet the Shale Gas Industry argue
the science is sound.

The Department of Energy and Climate Change
has given its approval,
for the systematic 'fracking'
for natural gas removal.
But hydraulic fracturing
is about smashing Earth's rock,
and our Government is allowing
this industry to run amok.

Using BTEX injections
of Benzene and Toluene,
of Ethylbenzene and Xylene.
A chemical hazard quite obscene.
Rupturing the aquifers
and polluting the water.
Disregard for the life underground
which they slaughter.

*Using millions of litres
of water under pressure.
Permitted exploitation
for unlimited measure.
Whilst humanity on the surface
is told there's a drought.
With the 'frackers' use of water
very soon there'll be nought.*

*The aquifers have been polluted
in Wyoming, USA.
And yet this has no bearing
on the decisions of today.
Damage to the water
occurred in Pennsylvania too.
Corporate denial of such evidence
sadly isn't new.*

*Earth tremors are more frequent
where 'fracking' has gone on.
The violent assault for Corporate gain
cannot continue on.
We must not be persuaded
that no harm is being done,
and we cannot give up opposing
until our case is won.*

We simply must protect our Earth
from these industrial vultures.
Preserving her resources
and beauty for all cultures.
Send your love to the Earth
to sooth her from quaking
and pledge from your hearts
to cease endless taking.

Vanessa Bristow-Rose

Creative Thought

Every thought and every deed
has its own unique creative seed.
Like vines they reach out into space,
their vibration felt by every galactic race.
All thoughts connect into the energy field sea,
their frequencies affecting the world that we see.

Reverberating through all the dimensions of time,
thoughts create a reality,
either destructive or sublime.
If the thoughts are of love toward all humankind,
gratitude to the Creator
and a giving attitude of mind,
then the glory of life and joy in our world,
will be the blessing we all can expect to behold.

Ego without compassion
germinates confrontational thought,
from which competitive attitudes
and separation is brought.
We must be guarded over the thoughts we allow,
if truly a new world we wish to create now.
For what we think is what we create.
Which is why our world has
so much judgement and hate.

The empowering understanding
is by seeing that we do...
as creators...
change our reality however we choose to.
We can decide that our Earth
will be honoured and blessed,
that all inequality be permanently addressed.
When we unite in a vision of Earth's restored glory,
then life for humanity will transform
into a joyous new story.

Sing With The Angels
(Lyrics)

<u>Chorus</u>
Sing with the Angels.
Sing a merry song.
Sing with the Angels
Loudly and strong.

Join with Archangel Michael and Raphael,
Archangels Uriel and Gabriel.
There's help in abundance,
our family are here.
Angels surround us,
there's nothing to fear.

Chorus

Our light must shine brightly here on the Earth.
Pure human love will assist our rebirth.
Boldly believe that
the Earth will have peace.
Once we are united,
all wars will cease.

Chorus

Vision a healing for all living things.
A new loving world
is what compassion brings.
I will love you
and you will love me.
Humanity united will set us all free.

Chorus

The Mouse And The Gnome

Once there was a little mouse
which lived in a brittle house.
A shoebox was its home sweet home,
which belonged to Fred, the gnome.

Together every day at four
they would clean the house and more.
First the mouse and then the gnome
would leave their house to be alone.

Around the hillsides, fields and lakes,
not much time it seems to take.
Fetching food and seeking friends
until quietly night descends.

As the sky is streaked with red,
two little figures go home to bed.
Once asleep the moon appears
and watches them with loving tears.

Through the night they soundly sleep
but wake before the sun will peep.
Once again they start their day
and we watch them laugh and play.

Rowena Bristow

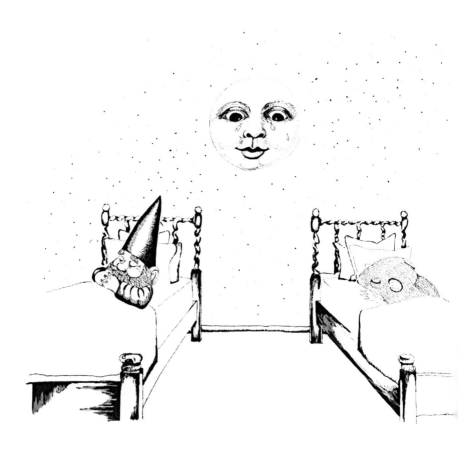

A Tree's Story Of Love

Midsummer...and the garden's lush
with leaves so fresh and green.
The little sapling stood centre stage,
her full beauty to be seen.
Around her, sculptured colourfully,
was nature at its best.
Pretty flowers of varied kinds
and a bush with a robin's nest.
For six years she had blossomed
pink 'candy floss' in Spring.
The little robin sat in her.
She so loved to hear him sing.

They came one day with a digger,
mechanical, loud and strong.
The roar and rattle concerned the tree,
she sensed something was wrong.
Silence fell upon the garden.
Nature quivered at their intent.
Just a bit of garden reconstruction
is what the humans meant,
but that would mean destruction.
Plants would have to die.
The price for cosmetic redesign,
was to Nature, far too high.
The digger grunted loudly
and advanced towards the tree.
She shook in fear and shouted,
"I'm living. Can't you see?!"
The ground heaved up.

The Lion Within

Roots snapped apart.
The little tree wept softly
within her heart.
The digger wrenched her
from out the earth,
her mother.......
since her seedling birth.
Roots injured, she sat in a plastic bag
in the heat of a summer sun,
barely any water,
her slow thirsty death had begun.
One week later her leaves had dropped.
Her essence faded.
Her heartbeat stopped.

Then gentle hands caressed her,
lifted her to a special spot.
Lovingly placed her in the ground
and watered her a lot.
The water had been blessed
with grateful loving thought.
And dying tree drank thirstily
every drop that it was brought.
Sacred geometric patterns
were strapped to slender trunk.
Before much time, new tree roots
had grown and deeply sunk.
When the first new leaf ventured out,
there was joyous celebration.
The gift of life had returned
from the tree's source of creation.
Love was daily showered upon her

and the tree responded
by growing stronger.
Proof came after two short years
that love heals
all our pain and fears.
The tree was keen
to show her gratitude and to give,
a gift of love
for helping her to live.
So with Spring's early sunny days,
pink 'candy floss' blossomed
at the touch of warm rays.
And the robin returns to the tree
in fine weather.
His pretty song reminds her
that a friend's love lasts forever.

Prayer

Love heals bodies
and love heals minds.
Love heals the memories
that a broken heart finds.

Love is the Divine breath
to help us grow.
Compassion is the nourishment
to help love flow.

When I Look Into Your Eyes

When I look into your eyes....

I see universes in countless number,
spiralling in the endless cycle of creation.
Life, in all its diversity, vastness and wonder,
stretching out beyond conceivable imagination.
Beautiful in its richness of form and colour,
I see sparks of life begin
from the Great Central Sun.
Later to dwell in the womb of the Earth Mother,
evolving into exotic varieties of being.
Yet all born of the ONE.
Each spark a universe of its very own,
a microcosm of the galactic macrocosm of might.
Each spark a divine illumination grown,
from the loving heart
of the Creator's pure light.
I see that you are that sacred, blessed spark,
a gift of bright light sent out from the Source,
with lives to experience,
adventures to embark.
Giving your soul an evolutionary ascension course,
all experiences assisting your soul's sacred journey.
Gathering knowledge to illuminate
what really is true.
That all life is meant to be in perpetual harmony,
connected forever in love.
You are me and I am you.

Poison Sky

As a child I would gaze at the cobalt blue sky,
so intensely beautiful,
it was a gift to the eye.
An occasional cloud might race across,
leaving no trace of the path it would cross.
Casually wondering how far I could see,
perhaps deep into the fathomless cosmic sea.
An uninterrupted view of Earth's sacred sky,
carried the dreams from my soul way up high.
The sun, radiantly and warmly, blessing my face,
and caressing Earth's garment
with gentle, soft grace.
Such blinding brilliance,
too intense to look.
Earth receiving the sun's probing,
in every cranny and nook.
Dots in the sky of planes traversing overhead,
oblivious to the sun's blessing, as onward they sped.
A small vapour trail, which soon vanishes away,
might sometimes appear from a plane making way.
Only for moments would this trail leave a scar,
disappearing suddenly like an early dawn star.
So how did we not notice the change in our sky?
It is time that we did,
then we can ask why......
all the criss-crossing of trails leaving milky white skies,
from horizon to horizon
with the sun screened from our eyes.
Deposited by aircraft whose identity is unclear,
a political motive, it would seem, might be here.

The Lion Within

Government is dismissive,
health risks are denied,
but the evidence would indicate
that they have all lied.
Geo-engineering is about manipulating the weather.
It seems governments and corporations
are working together.
Do chemtrails help humanity by blocking the sun?
Surely megatons of toxic material
cannot be good for anyone.
Aluminium, Strontium and Barium
from our skies fall,
raining down perpetually upon us all.
Chemicals in our water, our food and our air,
poisoning us slowly without
consideration or care.

Resist it we must!
Let our voices be heard!
A clear message that 'crop spraying'
is insanely absurd.
But we cannot get angry
and must try not to blame,
for love is the way to transform this corrupt game.
Our united heart resonance
creates a powerful vibration,
which will transmute all energies
of death and destruction.
To those full of harmony and loving creation,
we can transform all intentions
to harm and destroy,
by sending blessings to the chemtrailers
of pure love and joy.

Earth Angels

Earth Angels walk amongst us;
they take on human form.
They're here to help and guide us,
to help us weather all life's storms.
These beings of radiant, heavenly light
have folded their wings away,
to be incarnate here on Earth
to help souls find their way.

Earth Angels can pass unnoticed
for they come in many guises.
A relative, a friend, a stranger,
in all colours, shapes and sizes.
Their messages of comfort will
synchronistically cross your road,
delivered in many packages
to relieve or share your load.

Earth Angels emanate peace and light,
it helps to calm our fears,
and gently, with compassionate love,
they affectionately dry our tears.
These light-workers come in voluntary service,
which usually goes unseen,
never expecting gratitude for what
they've done or said or been.

The Lion Within

Earth Angels can find it hard
to adjust to Earth's dense and heavy plane.
The pull is strong to return
to the heavenly home again.
Yet still they long to come here
to help us all they can.
So when things fall in place for you
send all the gratitude you can.

I Win... You Lose

When a sport is practiced
for pleasure or fun,
then there is no harm
energetically done.
But raise the stakes
with celebrity status and wealth,
and the competitiveness quickly
becomes bad for our health.

Being better than another
is an illusion believed,
as for every one winner
many losers feel aggrieved.
With the pain of perceived failure,
the disappointment of losing,
this is when belief in one's self
suffers a bruising.

What achievement is there then
in the winner's story,
if hurting others is the trade
for a champion's glory?
Is it just another mechanism
for driving humanity apart?
The division causing fracturing
to our united heart.

Many systems have been built
to endorse the separation belief.
This untruth bringing us feelings
of isolation and grief.
The illusion we are individuals,
separate and alone.
'I win...you lose' is a belief seed
best not sown.

Perhaps our salvation
is in embracing each being's gifts.
Changing old beliefs
which have created such rifts.
Recognising the similarities,
that we're all 'cells' of the ONE.
Celebrate, instead, our uniqueness,
the beauty within everyone!

All That Is

A stone is a fragment of a far greater thing.
It's a piece of a mountain
with the same wisdom to bring.

A single grain of sand on any of Earth's beaches,
holds the essence of the waves
of the sea that it reaches.

Each leaf holds the memory of the tree it grew upon.
When physically separated,
the energy link lingers on.

Every flower petal bears the imprint of the whole.
It is the mirror of the flower's
eternal soul.

A fruit does not forget from where it came.
All its seeds have the blueprint
to replicate the mother plant again.

A drop of water is a part of the expressive expansive
sea,
always seeking reconnection
so at ONE it can be.

All trees of all species connect to one another,
all sharing the pleasure
and pain of each other.

Vanessa Bristow-Rose

We too are pure sparks of energy glowing bright,
part of the Source
of all divine light.
Woven within the field of 'All That Is',
created for co-existing
in eternal joyous bliss.

War Horse

A biological creation of strength.
A vision of power and might.
The horse, in all its glory,
is a creature of magnificence and light.
Here to show us our own true heart,
to be a friend both loyal and pure,
connected across all illusionary barriers
by a love that will endure.

This Being lives in harmony and peace.
Any threat perceived compelling flight.
We abuse this sensitive creature,
forcing it into battles that we fight.
The noise, the bombs and terror,
death always expectant in the air,
yet standing side by side with us
throughout the wars that we declare.

On the battlefields they have fallen
and thousands of them died.
Yet still, despite the stench of fear,
have stood valiantly by our side.
The blood of many horses
has soaked Earth's blessed soil,
mingled in amongst our own,
our sweat and battle toil.

War is not our natural action,
we are not designed to hate.
It is not our human nature
to destroy, but to create.
Losing sight of who we are
has brought us to a painful place.
This can be altered in an instant,
when Oneness we embrace.

The horse, a sentient being of light,
reminds us it is not too late.
We need not live in fear and dread,
this need not be our fate.
When we remember we are eternal,
light beings of love that's pure.
Invincible in the face of war
by a love that will endure.

Crop Circles

Acre upon acre lie golden fields,
orderly, regular and neat.
Gently swaying ripened heads
of waving, rippling wheat.
Nothing out of the ordinary,
nothing very strange.
Yet a curiously unusual phenomenon
exists within England's Wiltshire range.

In minutes the ripened crop
of rolling virgin canvas,
is blessed with sacred geometry
patterns, adorning the golden mass.
Stalks laid gently down
in swirl and curve and circle.
In such magnitude and intricacy,
it would appear to us a miracle.

Woven into symbols
to give the subconscious some direction,
of what we have forgotten
being incarnate in this dimension.
The love of 'All That Is'
and the nature of creation,
is imprinted in crop circle shapes,
to assist us toward ascension.
There is a vibration flowing
through Earth's agricultural scene.

Swirling, spiralling along
the ancient golden mien.
Underground, the water holds
cosmic creative power in deep,
and is stimulated by humanities
awakening from hypnotic sleep.

As frequencies of higher vibration
coincide in Earthly realm,
it's time for humankind to rise up
to take hold of freedom's helm.
To comprehend nature's messages
we need only extend our imagination,
then universal truths will be revealed
of our birth and all creation.

We can observe the geometric patterns
somehow elaborately created,
by forces not yet understood,
but the benefit of which...not doubted.
Though the conscious mind may question
and the meaning be unclear,
the resonance of the messages
our cells will certainly 'hear'.

Some say that men with planks and torches
creep into the fields at night,
making mathematically precise, giant shapes
whilst hidden from our sight.
Consider all the evidence
and then each of us can decide;
is it a hoax or is communication
coming to us from some other side?

Vanessa Bristow-Rose

The Spirit Of Yew

For sixteen hundred years
I have stood on this Earth,
growing in height,
in canopy breadth and girth.
I have watched over you gently
as the seasons passed by,
human life unfolding
in the twinkle of an eye.

Generations of children
tree climbing for fun.
Men discussing their errors
they wished were undone.
The maidens who dreamt
of the lover yet unseen.
And the old men who reminisce
on all that has been.

I have seen centuries of soldiers
boldly marching,
to later return demoralised,
injured or dying.
I weep to see the endless,
senseless waste.
Why do you destroy yourselves
with such thoughtless haste?

Why does your kind
feel driven to kill itself,
for the sake of status,
power and wealth?
I am old and still stand witness
to the cycles repeat,
each war another step
towards Humanity's defeat.

Each time you have touched me,
have sat down beneath,
ancient wisdom embraces.
All you need is belief.
It sings through my branches,
vibrates in the wood.
Please try to hear it.....
Oh, if only you would.

I whisper to you
of the divine glorious light,
of the wonder of creation,
pure love in plain sight.
All that is manifest
is Divine thought in form,
a gift of love eternal
to bless each Being born.

I am at one
with wind, sky and bird.
To think we are separate
is an illusion absurd.
The spirit of the Yew
is connected to you too.
For the Oneness of all
is the reality that is true.

The Lion Within

Vanessa Bristow-Rose

I Wonder Where You Are

I'm told you have dementia,
but to me that's just a name.
All I know is life has changed,
never again to be the same.
For some time I've felt you slipping away,
into a world apart from me.
The harder I try to reach you,
the more distant you seem to be.

Flickering moments of lucidity
and then I dare to hope,
but they say that this condition
is a downward slippery slope.
I understand so little
of the things that you now say,
witnessing ever decreasing quality
of your physical life each day.

I grieve your withdrawal
into a mind that is so muddled.
I agonise over how
you have painfully struggled,
to hold onto your dignity,
the personality that you are,
against a memory fading
until you forget who you are.

The Lion Within

You are lost and so confused,
your past is now a blur.
How much fear and anxiety
can your beloved body endure?
You are here amongst the living
yet I sense you're slowly dying.
When I'm with you
I can barely hold back from crying.

I'm holding your hand
but it feels like your soul's gone,
and truthfully I wouldn't want
your suffering to go on.
You walk around slowly,
your eyes stare ahead.
I wonder where you are,
so many tears I have shed.

Then one day a friend
gave this message to me.
She said "Do not grieve,
for your eyes cannot see.
The soul dwells in love,
compassion and glory.
Only the body lives out
this sad earthly story".

*Once re-united
with others on God's plane,
we learn that this difficult experience
brings us soul growth gain.
Whilst in this 'dream state'
the soul remembers its real essence,
and travels to higher dimensions
in its true 'I AM' presence.
There it helps angels
and the workers of light,
to heal Earth of karma
and assist her journey from the night.*

*So now when I look at you
I do so with humility
and with gratitude, for the service
you are giving to humanity.
Thank you my dearest,
beloved soul and friend,
now I try to see beyond the body.
Taking comfort now I know
for the soul there is no end.*

Earth's Child

Dear child of the Earth
please do not cry.
Your life seems in chaos
and you're wondering why.
You are a sovereign being
of divine cosmic light.
Freedom is your absolute
and inalienable right.

For you are a being
connected to the entire universe.
Yet there are an elite few,
who conspire to coerce,
you and your kind
into bondage for life.
This imprisonment creating
relentless agony and strife.

It's a clever entrapment
inflicted from your birth,
to enslave you for your lifetime
here on planet Earth.
Carefully contrived, to ensure
that you forget.
This battle for your consciousness
is not over yet.
When the veil of amnesia
lifts from human mind and eye,

then the chains of control crumble
and enslavement will die.
Laws are made to limit you,
things created for you to fear,
an invisible cage surrounds you,
hard to touch or see or hear.

Yet, the light that's deep inside you,
can see beyond the lies.
Truth cannot be hidden
from your inner loving eyes.
The love, when burning brightly,
within the human heart,
will break you free forever
and then the Golden Age will start.

Best Friend

I'd like to tell a story.
It is a heart warming tale,
about a wriggling ball of fluff
with paws and nose and tail.
How could I ever have foreseen
what this ball would grow to be,
and how, in time, this little dog
would mean all the world to me.

The memories are so many
but it's interesting to see,
that the little acts of naughtiness
are the fondest ones to me.
There's the time he chewed the sunglasses
and up the curtain peed.
Dragged my underwear down the garden.
Was this normal for the breed?

I took him off to classes
to learn a rule or two.
He treated it like a social club;
he wasn't being told what to do.
He looked so cute just sitting there
with eyes to make me melt.
He knew I loved him anyway.
He knew just how I felt.

Soul friends forever.
Love holding us gently together.

The Lion Within

A true best friend is one who's there
no matter what befalls,
and who forgives your darker side
and only ever the light recalls.
My doggie friend is faithful,
he is loyal through and through,
with a safe and never judging ear
I can trust any secrets to.

My dear beloved little dog
is the best friend that I've known,
and over time, since we first met,
our mutual love has grown.
He has always been dependable,
solid as a brick.
No matter what my own mood is,
I'd still be rewarded with a lick.

The moment came to say goodbye
to my little friend.
I could not stop from crying,
although I knew death was no end.
In the last look that he gave me,
love was in his eyes,
a love that lives eternal
even when the body dies.

Vanessa Bristow-Rose

Imagine

Imagine the barriers
between nations coming down.
Peace descending
over every city and town.
Armies being willing
to lay their guns down.....Imagine.

Imagine between people
a compassion and empathy,
an understanding of past suffering,
of forgiveness and sympathy.
The end to all
human created catastrophe.....Imagine.

Imagine no racism
and no class distinction,
no poverty, no thirst,
no hunger emaciation.
With enough food to share
we could eliminate starvation.....Imagine.

Imagine a world
where money didn't rule.
Where children could learn
real life gifts in school.
Where we embraced someone's difference
not made them a fool.....Imagine.

Imagine, if you can,
that we are all ONE,
like a single sacred breath
from the Great Central Sun.
Then we wouldn't dream of hurting
or killing someone.....Imagine.

We must remember we create
the reality we're in.
That loving intention will usher
the new Golden Age in.
Every human being equal and free.
So let's begin.....to imagine.

Vanessa Bristow-Rose

Death Towers

Dark metal towers,
skeletons against nature's sky.
Silent. Still. Feigning harmlessness
to all who pass by.
Displaying aerials and dishes,
attempting to disguise
what they really are,
whilst deceiving our eyes.
Smaller than a pylon
they often go unseen,
camouflaged to blend
into any urban or rural scene.
Individually located
in many scenic places,
out in the open
with their deceptively hidden faces.
Some are like telegraph poles,
alarm boxes or trees,
whilst all the time
triggering within us dis-ease.
Each tower emits waves
of microwave radiation,
all day and all night....
twenty-four seven.
We are electromagnetic Beings,
born out of sound,
resonance and vibration
into manifestation profound.
We live in a space
of flowing overtones and frequencies.
A plethora of sound

and other musical mysteries.
Most of them uplifting,
invigorating and harmonious,
but those from the towers
are intensely injurious.
Too much radiation
for our bodies to avoid,
overwhelmed...it's not long
before DNA is destroyed.
A thought for the police,
the paramedics and fire crew,
forced to accept Tetra Airwave,
Oh, if only they knew!
What power this mutant
communication system has
to deform human cells,
triggering tumours en masse.
Sold down the river
with no care for their health,
the Government supports industry
to pile up its wealth.
These 'Death Towers' have been proven
to make people ill,
to influence behaviour
so we act contrary to our freewill.
Beware of the sources of WiFi
and EMF radiation zones
from mobiles, Smart meters,
microwaves and dect phones.
It all seems quite hopeless,
but we have the power within
to use our compassion

to change everything.
United in love,
we will no longer entrain
to the lower vibration frequencies,
in a world that's insane.
Claim back our sovereignty!
Cease to consent to the sham
perpetuated by corporations
in their eugenics programme.
Our higher emotions
can overcome all of this,
return our cell status
to a level of bliss.
Get over the fear!
We're more powerful
than we think!
Heart resonance will heal all,
bringing us back from the brink.
We can unite our consciousness
for we are conduits of light,
thereby raising our vibration
and overriding corporate might.

What If....It's An Illusion?

What if....the world that we see
isn't actually real?
Not solid despite what we think,
see and feel.
Our limited five senses
convince us that it's there,
a physical reality
that each of us share.

What if....all that we see
is really condensed light,
a vibration slowed down
to appear in our sight?
Is the world a hologram,
a virtual reality game?
An experience for the mind,
within a matrix frame?

What if....the Earth is a stage
with plays all unfolding?
Each of us actors
in conscious unknowing,
robotically obeying
the governance created,
to divide and enslave us,
our development fated.

What if....an enlightened new world
of happiness and joy,
was ours to envision
for every girl and boy?
Simply forming an intention
so strong we could feel,
would manifest our dream
to make it become real.

What if....instead, we become
the observers of it all?
We could create a new play
to make tyranny fall.
We could vision for everyone
a world without lack.
Abundance for all
bringing paradise back.

What if....we are the film maker,
the author and playwright?
The power is within us
to bring the world right.
To shine light into darkness,
melt shadows away,
uniting people in love
to birth a new day.
Dissolve the illusion
that's kept us enslaved.
Our reward....a blue planet
we have lovingly saved.

The Lion Within

Ubuntu

(A Zulu word meaning...
I am what I am because of who we all are)

Under Ubuntu we can create for ourselves a new Earth,
where all beings are honoured for their individual
worth.

Become once again a planet of equal sharing,
with abundance for all and compassionate caring.

United we will evolve into a species at peace,
set free from suffering, triggering enslavement
release.

No longer controlled by the vice-grip of banks,
without money there will be no more missiles, guns
and tanks.

Treating each other with pure love and respect,
will have the enlightening, transforming effect.

Unity between nations, all races and tribes,
will ensure that our beautiful, blue planet survives.

"You never change things by fighting the existing
reality.
To change something, build a new model that makes
the existing model obsolete."
Buckminster Fuller

Only Love Resides Here

Over thousands of years
violent power struggles have been had
and the destruction of the Earth
devastatingly bad.
There is death in the air,
with pain everywhere.
The massacre of nations
our hearts ache to bear.

There is an energy that manipulates,
to control the human mind,
programming and suppressing,
using lies to blind.
Filling our thoughts
with hatred and violence,
creating a lack in our world
of love, joy and innocence.

Thoughts are like seeds,
they flourish and grow.
Anger and judgement
are not good seeds to sow.
Most beliefs have been planted
in our heads by another,
politicians, teachers,
friends, family or some other.

Some thoughts are creative,
loving and true.
Whilst others, like jealousy,
bring destruction to you.
Stop borrowing thoughts,
seek wisdom within.
The heart holds a truth
to bring enlightenment in.

This planet is a paradise,
nature lives in peace.
If we open our hearts
then all fighting will cease.
We've been tricked into thinking
we are beings apart,
forgetting we are all connected,
to the ONE loving heart.

The wisdom of the 'All That Is'
lies in every human heart.
Absolute truth dwells there
so it's a good place to start.
Then the external influences
will stop bringing us fear,
and we will see, that in truth,
only LOVE resides here.

Taking The Piss

There is an ancient therapy
for preserving your youth.
It will even reverse ageing
if you are 'long in the tooth'.
It's cheap and it's quick,
and it never runs out.
It can trim down the figure
if you're a little bit stout.

This elixir is incredible;
it will heal all your ills.
It does it so neatly
without any pills.
It's really quite simple,
you just have a pee.
Drink some urine yourself
and soon you will see.

Splash it on all over,
it's the real Eau De Toilette.
You may think I'm piss taking
but they might bottle it yet.
Your skin will be softer,
your hair nicer too,
but in the heat of the summer
the flies might like you!

You've heard of recycling
and you know that it's good,
but isn't urine therapy
taking it further than it should?
I fancy a fruit juice,
or water or wine,
but not wee in a glass
even though it is mine.

Don't flush it down the lavie,
this golden liquid treasure.
"Drink it twice a day", they say,
not a lot.....just in small measure.
It's a divine gift of medicine
for the rich and for the poor.
Our conditioned disgust
is why we don't drink it anymore.

So if you need healing
you could give the doctor up.
Summon your courage
and go to the karzy with a cup.
Bless this ancient secret
to escape the sickness smog.
Heal thyself through old advice,
"Go see a man about a dog"!

The Awakening Police

I'm a British Policeman;
I've joined the Constabulary.
It's a community responsibility
I'm willing to carry.
The appeal is to help people;
it's an honourable job,
catching law breakers
and those who burgle and rob.

As a British Policeman
I'm here to keep the peace,
to ensure the public
aren't violated or fleeced.
Justice and truth
are the beliefs that prevail,
to keep everyone safe
and the villains in jail.

I'm a British Policeman
intending to earn respect and thanks.
We're peaceful men and women
without missiles, guns or tanks.
Here to protect and help you,
just seek us out.
Find us patrolling in Panda cars
or beat-walking about.

I'm a British Policeman
using ancient Common Law.
Cause no harm and cause no loss,
covers everyone...rich and poor.
I've pledged my oath in service
to keep the people free,
to protect all life and property
and let the law abiding be.

Now I'm a Corporate Police Officer,
the times have marched on.
The old familiar ways
and public respect have gone.
We're members of a Police Force,
here to enforce company law.
It's about making profit,
not serving people anymore.

I'm a Corporate Police Officer
with new tools of trade.
More than handcuffs and truncheon
to make you afraid.
We're armed for rebellion
with tasers, teargas and guns.
Surveillance installed everywhere
so you can't hide or run.

The Lion Within

I'm a Corporate Police Officer
and I'm seeing treachery fermenting.
Within our walls, once symbols of trust,
crime is manifesting.
The Officers too are under attack
of which they are unaware.
The Tetra sets are making them ill.
It is done without due care.

I'm a Corporate Police Officer,
but I've opened my eyes.
The Police Service has been sold off
for Corporate enterprise.
The people are not terrorists;
Government is where
the tyranny hides,
manipulating police and people
to be on opposing sides.

Although I'm a Corporate Police Officer
I'm one of the people too.
Underneath the uniform,
I'm just like all of you.
With Tetra affecting all of us
the thing we need to do,
is unite, not be divided.
Then we'll not be dictated to.

I'm the Police Person that's awoken,
I'm here to stand for truth.
Here to speak for justice
for the elderly and the youth.
I see the crimes against humanity,
so with the people I will stand.
Together we will reinstate peace
throughout our towns and land.

Hector The Dragon

Now Hector was not a regular dragon.
His features were just not the norm.
His scaly skin was pearly white
like snow laid in a storm.
His eyes were not a smooth dark brown.
They were bluer than the sky.
His difference was a real concern.
He pondered on it.....
wondering why?
Hector was a friendly dragon
and he loved to play about.
But other dragons teased him
and often left him out.
So he was feeling lonely
and wished that he could be
just like all the others.
Not different. Do you see?
Hector could not appreciate
that he was a very awesome sight.
Brightly, all around him,
was a halo of glowing light.
He did not see that he was special.
He felt he was a freak.
To be the same and fit in
was all he tried to seek.
One day the wise old dragon came.
She had heard of Hector's light.
She had flown across
the forests and hills;
A full day and a night.
There was an ancient prophecy

about a white dragon being born,
at a new time for the planet
to signify arrival of its dawn.
A white dragon is a sacred Being,
the prophecy had said.
A sign that Christ Consciousness
had returned, to bless with life
what had been dead.
The Wise One called Hector to her.
He feared she might
send him away.
Because he was not normal
she might say he couldn't stay.
The Wise One smiled at Hector.
It soothed his nervous belly.
And when she kissed
his soft white head,
he shook like he was jelly.

"Hector, my dear,
there is no need for doubt.
Or the belief that you
are the odd one out.
Always look beyond the cover
to see the soul beneath.
The Tree of Life
has many branches
upon which we are each a leaf.
Know then, dear Hector,
soul of eternal light,
your beauty within
shines outwards rather bright.

A reminder to all of us,
here on the Earth,
that love is the pathway.
The vehicle for rebirth.
A messenger you are
from divine high places.
A vision of hope
for all of Earth's races".

Hector was full
of emotions of joy
and threw himself into the air.
His heart was bursting, and overflowing,
with abundant love to share.
So he wasn't a peculiar
oddity after all!
He would have to celebrate
with the dragons....one and all!
Now he remembered
what he came here to be...
a beacon of love
for all others to see.

Appendix

The Lion Within
It is my belief that there lives within all of us a power so strong that when used for the good it can move mountains. In unity, from this place, we can change the world.

"I was the shyest human ever invented, but I had a lion inside me that wouldn't shut up!"   *Ingrid Bergman*

Soul Of The Light
Is dedicated to Robert Green. A soul that has stepped into his power tirelessly in support of Hollie Greig and her mother. His voice has spoken out for Hollie's fight for justice and by doing so speaks for all children who are, or have been, victims of abuse. For further information see www.holliedemandsjustice.org and www.ukcolumn.org.

I'm Thinking Of You
A song written for my dear friend, Candice. Thank you for the times we shared. Love is eternal.

Communities Of Light
Please see Michael Tellinger's website www.michaeltellinger.com to read about Ubuntu Contributionism. Michael has written two books 'Temples Of The African Gods' and 'Slave Species Of God.' He is about to release a new book called 'Ubuntu Contributionism'.

Innit!
In the Thistle Chapel of St Giles Cathedral, Edinburgh there is a carving of an angel playing the bagpipes. This

poem is a light-hearted angelic interpretation of bagpipe players practice sessions.
'Innit' is a joke expression by my band colleague, Andy, which always makes me laugh!

<u>One Earth</u>
One of the inspirations for this poem is John Lennon's song 'Imagine' and especially the lyrics:-
> **"Imagine there's no countries**
> **It isn't hard to do**
> **Nothing to kill or die for**
> **And no religion too**
> **Imagine all the people**
> **Living life in peace..."**

<u>Jessie's Trust</u>
This is a small charity in East Sussex which raises funds for other small animal charities. For further information www.facebook.com/JessiesTrustAnimalSanctuary.

<u>What's This Fracking?</u>
A total abomination and violation of our divine Mother Earth. Haven't we reeked enough destruction already?
For further information readers can explore the following
www.dangersoffracking.com,
www.gaslandthemovie.com
Also on YouTube there is a lot of information on Hydraulic Fracking. Suggested viewing: 'Jessica Ernst, The Consequences of Fracking.'

<u>The Mouse And The Gnome</u>
A delightful poem written by my beloved sister, Rowena. She wrote this in 1977 and I'm sure never thought for a

moment that it might end up in print. She departed this world in 1995 at the age of 41 years. It is in memory of her physical life and in honour of her eternal light that I include her poem in this book. I love you dear sister.

A Tree's Story Of Love

This is a true story of a little flowering cherry tree which, one summer, was unceremoniously ripped out of the ground and left dying. It is a story demonstrating the power of love for the tree returned to full blossoming after being rescued by loving hearts.

Poison Sky

For more information check out two films on YouTube 'What In The World Are They Spraying?' and 'Why In The World Are They Spraying?'
There are many websites on the subject of chem trails. For example:-
www.uk-skywatch.co.uk,
www.toxicsky.org,
www.weatherwars.info,
www.coalitionagainstgeoengineering.org.
An interesting book on this subject is 'Angels Don't Play This Harp' by Dr Nick Begich and Jeane Manning.

War Horse

Inspired by the film of the same name. I watched the film during a long distance flight from Heathrow to San Francisco. It touched me so much that this poem was written whilst 33,000 feet up in the air!
According to www.wiki.answers.com *8,000,000 horses, on all sides, are believed to have died in the First World War.*

Crop Circles
There are many websites on this subject but a good place to start is www.lucypringle.co.uk and Bert Janssen's website www.cropcirclesandmore.com. He has also written a book called 'Sophia's Egg.'

I Wonder Where You Are?
This was a difficult poem for me to write. It was written whilst I was sitting in a Care Home next to someone dear to me who has dementia. I hope this poem may give some comfort to anyone who, like me, has someone they love suffering from dementia or alzheimer's.

The Spirit Of Yew
Trees inspire me. Especially very ancient ones. There is an old yew tree near where I live which carbon testing has established it to be 1600 years old. This wonderful tree has a commanding yet peaceful presence. This poem is in 'her' honour and in grateful recognition of the joyous gifts all the trees of Earth bring to humanity.

Best Friend
In loving memory of my dear friend, Dandy. A chocolate brown miniature poodle with the most amazing personality. I was blessed to have his companionship from 1999 to 2013. "Soul friends forever. Love holding us gently together."

Imagine
Another poem inspired by John Lennon and his famous song of the same name.
As relevant today as it was back then.

Death Towers

The effects of electromagnetic radiation from cell phone towers is something which affects us all. I invite you to look at the following.
www.mastsanity.org,
www.tetrawatch.net,
www.powerwatch.org.uk,
www.emfsensitivity.org
Also, very informative on YouTube is 'Resonance – Beings of Frequency.' There is masses more on the web you can research.

What If....It's An Illusion

An inspiration from reading David Icke's book 'Infinite Love Is The Only Truth. Everything Else Is Illusion.'
www.davidicke.com

Ubuntu

Ubuntu is a Zulu word meaning "I am what I am because of who we all are." To read more about the Ubuntu Contributionism System please see Michael Tellinger's website www.michaeltellinger.com.
Also view www.ubuntuparty.org.za *– 'Unity and Higher Consciousness for a New World.'*

Taking The Piss

There are many books you can research into on the subject of Urine Therapy. Here are some suggestions:
'The Water Of Life' by John W. Armstrong.
'The Golden Fountain, The Complete Guide to Urine Therapy' by Coen van der Kroon.
'Your Own Perfect Medicine' by Martha M. Christy.

The Lion Within

The Awakening Police

This poem is reflecting the evolution of the Police Service from the perspective of someone who has worked within it.

It is an invitation also to the well meaning men and women who work there still to awaken to the health threat of Tetra (Terrestrial Trunked Radio).

For more information please see the following.

www.mastsanity.org,

www.tetrawatch.net,

www.powerwatch.org.uk,

www.emfsensitivity.org

Lightning Source UK Ltd.
Milton Keynes UK
UKOW04f2333110714

234974UK00001B/29/P